Original title:
The Life of a Leaf

Copyright © 2025 Creative Arts Management OÜ
All rights reserved.

Author: Christian Leclair
ISBN HARDBACK: 978-1-80581-745-1
ISBN PAPERBACK: 978-1-80581-272-2
ISBN EBOOK: 978-1-80581-745-1

Graciously Undone

Once a sprout with dreams so grand,
Winds kicked me out, I hit the land.
I spun and twirled, a dizzy dance,
My graceful fall became my chance.

Leaves laughed as I took a dive,
They whispered, "Hey, it's great to thrive!"
But on the ground, I made my mess,
A crunchy pile of leafiness.

The Anatomy of a Falling

A little leaf dressed up in green,
Thought gravity was just a dream.
One gusty day, it took a plunge,
And heard the trees applaud and grunge.

It wobbled, jiggled, what a sight,
Flipped and flopped, oh what a flight!
A dance with fate, a spin, a drop,
And finally landed – a leaf's grand flop!

Sunshine Slants and Shadows

Sunshine hit me square in the face,
Said, "Hey there, spark up the place!"
I shimmered bright and buzzed like mad,
But shadows lurked, looking quite sad.

"I need a break!" groaned one old shade,
"I'm tired of all this leaf parade!"
"Just hang on tight, we'll sway with glee,
Let's make the most of this sunny spree!"

Leaves Paving Paths

In autumn's chill, we took our stand,
A carpet bright across the land.
People walked and gave a cheer,
"What a path! Let's dance right here!"

We rustled and crunched, all in play,
"Who knew we'd brighten up their day?"
Rolled on the ground, created trails,
Laughing at folks in silly gales.

Pilgrimage of Parting

A leaf set off on a bold quest,
Flapping bravely, never at rest.
With a gust in tow and a twirl in flight,
It dodged the dog's mouth—what a sight!

Bidding farewell to the sturdy old tree,
"It's been quite a ride, just you and me!"
But the wind had a giggle, a gleeful laugh,
As our leafy friend flopped into the path.

Down to the ground with a clumsy thud,
Joining a pile—oh, what a crud!
"Here's to the colors!" it did cheer,
"But give me some gas for my next frontier!"

So off it swirled, through puddles and mud,
Making new friends in a leaf litter flood.
"A pilgrimage of parting, a show of grace!"
It grinned with joy, in this silly space.

Strokes of the Seasons

In spring, a bud poked out and grinned,
But winter's return made it rescind.
It danced with the daffodils, full of cheer,
Then sighed as each blossom disappeared.

Summer brought sun, a chance to frolic,
With picnics and parties, life was so volatile.
Jostling with bugs on a sunbeam's floor,
But then came the rain—who asked for more?

The fall showed up with a colorful twist,
"Look at us, all reds! We're artists, not mist!"
But the wind had other plans in its scheme,
And swiftly scattered them, as if in a dream.

Yet through it all, the leaf learned to sway,
With every new gust, it knew how to play.
Embracing each season, with laughter and tease,
A jester of nature, dancing with ease!

Whispers of Autumn's Embrace

In a tree high above, a chatter unfolds,
Leaves giggle and gossip, their tales never old.
They fashion a cap for the squirrel with glee,
"Try this, it's stylish! Just wait till they see!"

They swirl in the breeze, like a playful parade,
Each pirouette perfect, no grace left to invade.
"Watch my bold flip!" one leaf shouts with delight,
Yet lands in the puddle, oh what a sight!

A Journey in Green

Once a tiny bud held dreams of grand sights,
"I'll dance on the breeze!" it exclaimed with delights.
But as summer raged with its sun-shining pranks,
It found it was stuck in a band of rank ranks.

"Oh woe!" cried the leaf, "Where's my freedom to float?
I'm ready for travel!" with a silly little gloat.
But the wind shook its head, "You've got time to spare,
Just hang on tight, buddy, I'll take you up there!"

Fluttering Memories of Fall

With colors so bright, they a'flutter like birds,
Leaves reminisce tales, all sprinkled with words.
"Remember last spring, when we danced in the rain?
Then chilled with the frost, not a moment of pain!"

Fall grinned and stretched, as the days turned to gold,
"Let's spin 'round in circles—be brave, we're bold!"
But one leaf fell down with a comical thud,
"I meant to do that!" it said, back to the mud!

The Dance of Days Gone By

As seasons would change, the leaves laughed in rows,
"Remember that time we wore snows like our clothes?"
With each twirl and twist, through the air they would play,

"Then ended up stuck on a kid's car all day!"

They plotted and planned for the next big event,
"Oh, let's prank the trees! They've been too content!"
But a wise old branch said, with a wink and a wave,
"Careful, my friends, for it's trouble you'll crave!"

Patterns of the Perishing

Fell from the tree with a flurry of glee,
Spinning and twirling, oh look at me!
But when the dog jumped, oh what a sight,
I fluttered away, I was gone in a flight.

Crunching and munching, the snails had a feast,
They laughed at my fate, oh what a beast!
I scared all the kids with my brown, crunchy form,
Yet here in the mulch, I'm safe and warm.

The Embrace of Winter's Grasp

Winter's chill came nipping my toes,
Wrapped in a snowflake, I struck a pose.
I thought I was stuck, frozen so tight,
Until a squirrel came, and what a delight!

He grabbed me for fun, for a cozy old throw,
Warmed me up quick with a funny little show.
But when he got chilly, back on the ground,
I danced in the breeze, my freedom I found.

Nature's Golden Memoir

Once I was green, a bright little teen,
Now I'm golden and crispy, a sight seldom seen.
The wind gave a chuckle, it played with my hair,
Darting and spinning, oh what a flair!

A gust whistled low, I returned to the ground,
My friends said, 'you look like you've finally browned!'
I giggled and beamed, oh the stories I weave,
In this crazy old world, I refuse to grieve.

The Sway of Silent Stories

Under the moonlight, I fluttered with glee,
Sharing my whispers with a nearby tree.
While crickets played tunes, I did a little jig,
Twirling with joy, feeling quite big!

Then came the rain, a surprise to us all,
I danced in the droplets, oh what a ball!
But then with a plop, I found myself down,
A soggy old leaf with a soggy old frown.

Decay Diplomat

Once green and proud, I twirled on high,
Now I'm crinkled, waving goodbye.
Negotiating with the breeze,
Can't decide if I want to sneeze!

In my prime, I wore the crown,
Now I'm just a crunchy gown.
At the foot of trees, I lay down flat,
Sipping tea with a passing rat.

I was a fan to the sunlight's score,
Now I'm more of a dusty floor.
Tales of wind and laughter shared,
With squirrels who never cared!

With a chuckle, I let go,
To the ground, it's quite a show.
I may be wilting, but don't you fret,
I'm the life of the compost yet!

The Sway of Silent Stories

Under the moonlight, I fluttered with glee,
Sharing my whispers with a nearby tree.
While crickets played tunes, I did a little jig,
Twirling with joy, feeling quite big!

Then came the rain, a surprise to us all,
I danced in the droplets, oh what a ball!
But then with a plop, I found myself down,
A soggy old leaf with a soggy old frown.

Decay Diplomat

Once green and proud, I twirled on high,
Now I'm crinkled, waving goodbye.
Negotiating with the breeze,
Can't decide if I want to sneeze!

In my prime, I wore the crown,
Now I'm just a crunchy gown.
At the foot of trees, I lay down flat,
Sipping tea with a passing rat.

I was a fan to the sunlight's score,
Now I'm more of a dusty floor.
Tales of wind and laughter shared,
With squirrels who never cared!

With a chuckle, I let go,
To the ground, it's quite a show.
I may be wilting, but don't you fret,
I'm the life of the compost yet!

Hues of Hope and Despair

I started green with envy bright,
Flirting with the sun's warm light.
But now I'm a maroon, won't you see?
Feeling like I'm losing my degree!

Once a star in summer's glow,
Now I'm falling, taking it slow.
Orange giggles, as I drift down,
Trading laughs with a startled clown.

In every hue, a secret's told,
Of autumn dreams and winds so bold.
A leaf's romance? A funny tale,
Swaying gaily in the gale!

So here I dance, on the ground, laid low,
Colors of despair, but don't you know?
For in decay, I'm still quite fab,
Turning my brown tragedy into a jab!

Autumn's Final Waltz

In the brisk air, we spin and whirl,
With every gust, it's quite a swirl.
Oh, how I twirl in this grand ballet,
Falling like I'm auditioning today!

Rustling 'round with a cheeky grin,
Each spin is a chance for a win.
Caught off guard by a daring squirrel,
I'm the star of this autumnal whirl!

As I drift down, I hear the song,
Of seasons laughing, all day long.
With every twist, I take my chance,
In this leaf tango, let's advance!

So here I drift, to the earth I bow,
With a final twist, I'll take a bow.
Life's a jest, so let me prance,
In autumn's final waltz, I'll dance!

In the Cradle of Change

Cradled tight by the winds of fate,
I giggle softly, who can relate?
Once a giddy green, now a shade of brown,
I'm the talk of the town, as I tumble down.

The tree said, 'Fly!', with a flick of flair,
So here I am, dancing in midair.
With every flip, I spread my cheer,
Best leave my worries, it's time to veneer!

With crunchy pals, I'll lay to rest,
Finding joy in being the best.
For in this cradle, I play all day,
Making the most of my leafy ballet.

So tip your hats, as I hit the ground,
A clown in disguise, and laughter is found.
In a pile of ruckus, together we'll grin,
A festival of change, let the fun begin!

The Quietude of Becoming

Once a tiny bud on a tree,
I stretched my limbs just to be free.
But then a breeze shook my little frame,
And I thought, 'This isn't quite the same.'

Wiggling in the sunlight's dance,
I swayed around, given a chance.
But was that a squirrel, or was it a cat?
I froze in place—hey, now! Look at that!

While I twirled in seasonal grace,
I gathered many a bug's embrace.
Each one said, 'Oh, what a nice green,
You should join the circus; you're quite the scene!'

But as time passed, I turned a bit ripe,
And soon I could feel my leaf-like type.
With autumn's wink, I found my fate,
A comic tumble—uh-oh, here comes that plate!

Reflections of Shades and Seasons.

In spring I wore a bright, shiny hue,
Poking out like I just came through.
My buddies laughed, 'What a silly sight!'
But I felt fabulous, all sparkly and bright.

As summer approached with a sunny grin,
I felt the heat on my leaf-like skin.
A bird landed near, gave me a peck,
And I quacked back, 'Hey! Show some respect!'

With fall came a wardrobe change, oh my!
I donned rusty orange, sipping pumpkin pie.
The critters giggled, passing by my stand,
'You flip through colors like a painted band!'

But winter whispered, 'Time to take a rest!'
And down I crumpled, quiet, and blessed.
'No worries now, my green days are past,
Now I'm a funny memory that's made to last!'

Whispers of the Falling

From the top of a tree, I looked down below,
The world spun fast, and down I would go.
With each gust of wind, I took to my flight,
Shouting, 'Watch out, folks! I'm headed for fright!'

Tumbling and swirling, a leaf on the breeze,
I landed quite softly, oh, what a tease!
The ground said, 'Welcome! Take a seat care-free.'
'I didn't choose this! It chose me!' Oh, woe is me!

Gathering round, a heap of my kin,
We had a party—let the fun begin!
Splashed by some rain and the sun's warm kiss,
We rolled around, oh, what joy! Pure bliss!

But hey, what's this? A child came near,
To scoop us up with a giggle and cheer.
I thought they'd build a grand leaf pile so tall,
But turned out I became just a hat for a doll!

Vibrant Vein Chronicles

Every vein on me tells a sweet tale,
Of wind and of sun, and a very big snail.
I think of the dances and all of the fun,
'Til a raindrop falls, and I'm suddenly done!

With patterns designed like a marvelous map,
I showed off my beauty, took a little nap.
Yet sometimes a breeze gives my edges a tug,
'Not too tight, okay? Don't give me a shrug!'

Each passing day, I felt somewhat sassy,
But oh! My bright colors made me quite classy.
Then came a storm that decided to play,
I's whirled in a twirl—like ol' ballet!

Now I lie crumpled, a crinkly pile,
With memories tucked in, oh, what a style!
Though I slouch for now, here's my final decree:
'I may once have soared, but I'll always be me!'

Fluttering Farewells

I danced on a breeze, felt quite grand,
Twirling and spinning across the land.
Then came a gust, oh what a show!
A tumble, a trip, to the ground I go.

My friends in the trees waved goodbye in jest,
As I settled down, taking my rest.
A squirrel looked up, gave a cheeky grin,
'That's one less leaf for the trouble we're in!'

I tried to stay put, but the wind had a plan,
It blew through my veins like a rambunctious fan.
I flipped and I flopped, a ridiculous sight,
'The ground is my stage, let's dance with delight!'

So here I lay; watch me shine and twirl,
As critters below plot and squirrel.
To be just a leaf is a curious fate,
But oh what a laugh, it's never too late!

The Story Beneath the Bark

Under the bark lives a tale so bright,
With whispers of laughter that fill the night.
The ants throw a party, all snappy and neat,
With crumbs from the picnic a real tasty treat.

They dance in the shadows, a conga so spry,
While I, just a leaf, watch them float by.
A beetle crashed in with a clumsy quake,
'Excuse me, dear leaf, was that your mistake?'

The woodpecker taps to a rhythm so fine,
And I giggle away, oh how I do shine!
Each creature a character, in joy they confine,
While I sway in the breeze, good times intertwined.

As stories unfold in the bark's nightly glee,
I'd laugh out loud if I were more free.
For life in the forest spins endless and wild,
And I'm but a spectator, whimsical and mild!

Echoes of the Forest Floor

On the forest floor, oh what a sight,
Mushrooms play hide-and-seek, quite a delight.
With shadows that wiggle and giggles that gleam,
As I lay here, thinking, this must be a dream!

A rabbit hops by with a hop-skip-and-jump,
Tripping on acorns, oh what a clump!
'That leaf's in the way!' squeaks out a mouse,
As the forest erupts like a full-blown house!

Every rustle and shuffle tells stories anew,
From the flowers so bold to the skies oh so blue.
And here I giggle, part of the fun,
While the world moves along, under moon and sun.

So if you hear laughter amidst the tall trees,
It's creatures of mischief! Come join if you please.
For life is a dance, and we're all in the fray,
Just echoes that bounce, in a captivating play!

From Bud to Earth

I sprouted with style, green as can be,
Waving to the flowers, so fancy and free.
The insects all cheered, threw me a bash,
'Let's party all day! Let's make quite a splash!'

But soon I grew tired of the butterfly waltz,
As caterpillars grinned, 'It's not our fault!'
With stunts that failed and spins that went wrong,
I laughed at their antics, they couldn't be strong!

Then came a storm, and I swayed to and fro,
With raindrops a-tapping, now put on a show!
I flung with the wind, a crazy old flight,
'Hey world, look at me! I'm a leaf in delight!'

And when I let go, what a glorious fall,
I landed on soil, the best seat of all!
Now seeds gather 'round, ready for mirth,
Like me, when they sprout, they'll show what they're worth!

Lessons in Letting Go

Once I hung on, bright and green,
But the wind said, "Look, it's time to lean!"
With a swish and a swirl, I took my flight,
A tumble into the day, such a silly sight!

I danced with the breeze, so carefree and wild,
Like a toddler at play, with laughter compiled.
The ground was my stage, oh what a show!
Who knew falling could feel like a glow?

Each twirl, a lesson, with nature as guide,
Life's just a circus, come join for the ride!
Letting go isn't sad, it's a trip full of cheer,
Just look at me spinning, I've nothing to fear!

So if you're feeling clipped, don't be so bleak,
Just sway with the rhythm, and give it a tweak.
Life's not just hanging, it's bold and it's bright,
Be a leaf in the wind, take off in your flight!

Secrets of the Shimmering Canopy

Up high in the sun, we shimmer and sway,
With gossamer whispers, for all to relay.
We gossip with the breeze, oh what a delight,
Swapping tales of the bugs who buzz in the night!

Is that a small spider, spinning tales made of thread?
Or a squirrel with his dreams of a nut-filled spread?
We giggle and chuckle, it's quite the grand scene,
In our leafy realm, we reign as the queen!

Caught in the sunlight, we dance with such grace,
Every flicker a memory, every shade has a face.
Small joys of the branches, we lift up our voice,
Living together, it's simply by choice!

So wave at the sky with a flick and a twist,
For life in the canopy is too good to resist.
With laughter and friendship, we flourish and grow,
Secrets of shimmer, in our leafy cabaret show!

A Tantalizing Turn

I took a deep breath, stood tall and proud,
The world was my stage, a leafy shroud.
A flip in the air, oh what a surprise,
I twirled and I spun, under bright sunny skies!

A gust tickled softly, it whispered my name,
"Join me for a dance, let's lighten the game!"
With a twirl and a whirl, I answered the plea,
A skip in my step, oh how fancy I'd be!

Round and around, like a leaf in full glee,
I pranced through the air, as happy as can be.
My friends laughed along, in their dazzling attire,
A waltz with the wind took us higher and higher!

So if you're feeling stuck, take that tantalizing turn,
Dance with the breeze, let your spirit discern.
Life's a fun ride, just let out a cheer,
Be a leaf on the edge, let go of your fear!

In the Shadow of Giants

Among the tall trees, I wiggled with glee,
They towered above, so grand and free.
In their shadows I played, like a kid in a park,
With giggles and rustles, I left my own mark!

They'd whisper sweet secrets, of days long gone,
While I tossed down small jokes, oh what a con!
"Why did the acorn cross the road?" I'd cry,
"To grow up like you, what a big root, oh my!"

We'd chuckle together, roots all in a twist,
As sunshine would sparkle, we couldn't resist.
To bounce in the breeze, was a sight to behold,
The giants above me, with stories untold!

So if you find shade in a giant's embrace,
Join in the laughter, and pick up the pace.
For in every leaf, there's magic to share,
Life's best when you play, without any care!

An Unwritten Eulogy

In spring, I danced, a vibrant sprite,
Whirling in breezes, oh what a sight!
But autumn came, with gusts so bold,
And off I went, my story told.

The squirrels took aim, what a surprise,
With acorns they dropped, oh how I rise!
With laughter I twirled, through skies so blue,
Until I learned, I'm just flying stew!

Friends shouted, 'Look! A leaf on the run!'
'Try to catch me,' I said, 'It's all in good fun!'
So with every gust, I let out a cheer,
In this silly ballet, I've nothing to fear.

So raise a glass, for those that did fall,
We've had our laughs, and we gave it our all!
Let's remember the joy, the spins and the glide,
In this unwritten tale, I've nothing to hide.

Shades at Twilight

When daylight fades and shadows peek,
I play hide and seek, as the crickets squeak.
I'm a vestige of green, in a fading light,
A comedic act, ready to take flight!

The bugs buzz by, with a curious hum,
I'm thinking of pranks, like a leaf-made drum!
With twirls and flips, I tease the night,
For in this big show, I'm the star, quite right!

With gusts of wind, I take a bow,
The crowd of stars laughs, oh look at me now!
Twirling in rhythms, my green shades aglow,
A comedic encore, in twilight's soft flow.

As darkness settles, the moon gives a grin,
I leap from the branch, let the fun begin!
For as long as I flutter, I'll bring forth delight,
In this whimsical twilight, all banter feels right.

Between Branches and Briars

Among the thorns, I find my way,
Perched on a branch, where I want to play.
A giggle escapes as I take a dive,
Wiggling and jiggling, oh to be alive!

I'll ride on a breeze, like it's a fair ride,
And flip over hedges with glee, arms wide!
With spiders on strings and birds doing flips,
We dance through the thicket, all smiles and quips!

Nature's circus, oh what a sight!
With laughter and pranks, we own the night.
I'm a bold little leaf, taking chances galore,
A ruckus we make, that's what friends are for!

Through branches and briars, we frolic with flair,
Woven in laughter, no worries or care.
For every turn taken, a story to share,
In this colorful life, nothing can compare!

Nature's Fleeting Narrative

A tale written small, in hues of green,
I flutter and flounce, like a fantastical queen!
With whispers from winds, I craft my own spin,
In the theater of trees, oh let the fun begin!

With nibbled edges, I bear the new hues,
Like a patchwork of laughter, in morning's soft dew.
My memoirs are scattered, on sidewalks below,
With giggles and flutters, I steal the show!

I'm a slapstick star, in this narrative wide,
With every gust, I'm on another ride.
Fleeting my time in the sun, oh so fleet,
Caught in the wind, oh isn't it sweet?

So when I do fall, with a chuckle and cheer,
Know I'll return, as the seasons draw near.
For my story keeps swirling, in circles and loops,
Nature's own tale, with all its goofs!

Soliloquy of the Saplings

In the shadow of a giant oak,
Saplings scheme, and giggle, joke.
"What's it like up there so tall?"
"Do you get lost in leaves, or fall?"

The wind whispers tales, oh so grand,
Of daring leaps, a brave leaf band.
But roots are tangled, stuck in clay,
"Let's just pretend we're free today!"

They stretch and yawn, with dreams to soar,
While ants march on, a leafy chore.
"Just wait! One day, we'll join the dance!"
"Until then, let's just take a chance!"

With every drop of rain that falls,
They laugh and joke in lively brawls.
"If we sway hard enough, we might,"
"Become the stars in moonlit night!"

Embracing Autumn's Embrace

As summer waves goodbye with flair,
Leaves giggle, toss their colors in the air.
"Orange, yellow, who will win?"
"I'll take purple! Let's begin!"

They swirl and twirl in wind so bold,
While squirrels hoard their acorns, gold.
"C'mon! Join us in this fun!"
"Or are you all just out for a run?"

With each gust, they pirouette low,
"Hey, look at me! I'm nature's show!"
And when they land with a gentle thud,
They laugh, for autumn is a muddy flood!

While autumn makes the trees surrender,
The leaves keep dancing, full of splendor.
"We'll dress the ground, a fancy gown,
Now let's all celebrate the town!"

Dreams in a Green Veil

Underneath a sunlit sky,
Little leaves whisper, oh so sly.
"What if we could fly away?"
"Up to the clouds, let's go and play!"

They wiggle on their branches tight,
Imagining a wild, carefree flight.
"I'll be the captain, you my crew!"
"Swabbing decks of morning dew!"

Each flutter feels like a grand parade,
As young buds dream of adventures made.
"Let's race the birds, try not to crash!"
"Your leaves are green, mine's just a splash!"

In secret groups, they hatch a plan,
"To trip on raindrops—can we, can?"
With laughter echoing through the trees,
They embrace their dreams with oaky knees!"

Tides of Time in Green

Time flows like sap, sweet and slow,
Leaves gossip about the seeds they sow.
"Oh, remember when we were just buds?"
"Now we're stars, spinning in thuds!"

They chat of storms, of sun's warm grace,
Of raindrops' race, a splashing face.
"When autumn shows, and colors fade,
We'll dive into the leaf pile parade!"

"I'll wear a crown, you be my king!"
"Let's twist and twirl in nature's ring!"
Through seasons' tide, they've danced their way,
With every breeze, the leaves still play!

And when at last they touch the ground,
They giggle softly, round and round.
"We did it, guys! From green to gold,
What a story, forever told!"

The Dance of Life and Decay

In spring I sprout, so fresh and green,
My friends and I, a lively scene.
We twirl and spin, caught by the breeze,
Laughing at squirrels, doing as we please.

But time goes on, the sun does shine,
I gold and crinkle, my fate aligns.
The dance is slower, but that's no crime,
A twist, a bend, I'm still in my prime!

With each gusty gale, I hit the ground,
My friends are falling all around.
We giggle softly, it's quite the spree,
As they pile atop, enjoying our glee.

In the big brown pile, we find our glee,
Stories of summers sung merrily.
Life's just a dance, even in decay,
With laughter echoing day by day.

Memories in a Spiral

Swirling down from lofty heights,
I spin and twist in joyful flights.
With each twirl, I recall the sun,
Dancing days and so much fun!

A memory here, a chuckle there,
Chasing critters, none a care.
I made a hat for a muddy dog,
Oh, what a sight! A leafy bog!

The breeze whispers secrets, tales of yore,
While stomping feet, they beg for more.
But as I spiral, a thought does creep,
Will anyone remember? My heart takes a leap.

Yet down below, a child does grin,
Kicking my friends, oh let the fun begin!
In laughter and joy, the circle's complete,
Memories and spirals, oh what a treat!

An Autumn's Tale of Transformation

I start out green, a vibrant sight,
Then comes the fall, what a fright!
With hues of rust and golden flair,
I strut my stuff without a care.

Dancing on branches, life's in bloom,
Mocking the pumpkins, doom and gloom.
"Look at me, I'm trendy!" I shout,
While squirrels are busy, running about.

But one fateful day, a wind did blow,
Off I tumbled, down I go.
"Catch me if you can!" I laugh with glee,
A chase for the critters, oh what a spree!

Now on the ground, I take a seat,
In a pile so cozy, oh, isn't it sweet?
Transformations come, but don't you fret,
For autumn's tale is not done yet!

Nature's Brief Interlude

I'm here for a moment, a fleeting scene,
Caught in the charm of forest green.
With chittering critters and a sunny ray,
Oh, how I love the liveliest play!

A wink from a worm, a nod from a bee,
Swirling and twirling, wild and free.
"Look at me!" I boast, in the sunny glade,
As the world around me starts to fade.

The dance grows slower, I'm losing my grip,
Now I'm a rug on the forest trip.
Through laughter and joy, I accept my fate,
Lying in silence, so calm and sedate.

But wait! Here comes a child with glee,
Scooping me up for their grand spree!
Nature's brief interlude, a bubbly ride,
In laughter and joy, there's nothing to hide.

Whirls of Wistful Whispers

In summer's sway, I gleefully dance,
Waving at kids, oh what a chance!
Twists and jumps in a sunlight spree,
But gravity's pull says, 'Come here to me!'

A gust comes by, I take a spin,
Who knew the wind could be a friend?
Round and round, I go with glee,
In this airy whirl, I'm wild and free!

Tucked in a pocket, I start to hide,
Pretending I'm just a leaf with pride.
Then out I pop, to say "Hello!"
The giggles erupt, what a fine show!

But evening falls, I start to fade,
All those good times now played and laid.
Yet here I stay, in tales we weave,
Oh, the fun we had, this leaf, I believe!

A Leaf's Testament

I once was green, so lush, so bright,
Swaying gently in morning light.
Then summer came, a party divine,
With squirrels and bees, all friends of mine!

We'd hold grand feats, in the sun's warm smile,
Competing with clouds, oh we had style!
But as I twirled, a storm brewed near,
Typical drama — let out a cheer!

Fell to the ground, 'twas quite the sight,
Landed on dirt, 'What a wild flight!'
Caterpillars laughed, "It's a new kind of fun!"
As I danced with the ants, oh how they run!

Now autumn's here, I'm crunchy and brown,
Remembering shenanigans, never a frown.
Though I may be down, my spirit stays high,
In the hearts of all, I continue to fly!

Rustling Reminisce

Up in the tree, I didn't stay still,
Riding the breezes, such a wild thrill!
With each little shudder, a silent shout,
'Catch me if you can!' I'd twist and clout!

Then came a kid with bright, eager eyes,
Swung his arms wide — oh, what a surprise!
A poke, a prod, I flitted away,
Into a puddle, oh what a play!

I danced on the wind like I owned the show,
Tickled by raindrops, embracing the flow.
'Is that laughter I hear?' I'd ask with a grin,
'Or just the breeze whispering tales of the win?'

As I drift to the ground, now wrinkled and worn,
I'll cloak little creatures, with nature's adorn.
Filled with retreat, but not far to roam,
In every sweet rustle, I call this home!

Floating in the Fickle Winds

Oh, what a party, this floating affair,
Gliding on currents, without a care!
I swoosh and I swirl, but watch for the snag,
That sneaky old branch, oh what a drag!

With each twist and turn, I laugh out loud,
Ducking and diving, a leaf in a crowd.
'Catch me quickly!' I shout to the breeze,
As I tickle the tops of the tall, swaying trees!

Fickle the gusts that try to mishap,
They nudge me this way, then nudge me that lap.
But watch out, dear passerby on the ground,
I might land on your head, without making a sound!

Yet here I smile, in my autumn dress,
Telling my stories with an orange finesse.
Laughter will linger, 'till the next spring cheer,
When I'll dance once again, without any fear!

Echoing the Seasons

A leaf woke up, feeling spry,
It danced with gusts, oh my, oh my!
Flipped and flopped, did a tiny jig,
Hoping for summer, but got a twig.

In autumn's chill, it donned a coat,
With colors bright, it learned to gloat.
But winter came, and off it flew,
A snowball fight? Between branches too!

Spring arrived, it had to sprout,
With raindrops laughing all about.
gathered with friends in the sun's light,
They played all day, what a delightful sight!

Seasons passed, they waved goodbye,
From tree to ground, it gave a sigh.
But laughter echoed, never to cease,
For every fall brings new release.

Heartbeats Beneath the Branches

A leaf lay dormant, feeling quite lost,
Who knew gold could come with a cost?
Tickled by winds, it giggled around,
"I'm nature's confetti, flying unbound!"

But with every twirl, its friends did moan,
"Hey, don't forget, you're not alone!"
"We cling for warmth, we dance and sway,
While you play hopscotch with the sun's ray!"

With the sun's blushing, it turned quite bold,
"Let's paint the sky! It's getting old!"
They splashed on colors, a leafy spree,
"Oh look, I'm a rainbow!" said one with glee.

But as time passed, the giggles slowed,
A whisper of wind, "Time to unload!"
Yet, under the branches, a joy was stored,
Memories of laughter forever adored.

A Tapestry of Time

Once a sprout, so soft and small,
Folded in dreams, it danced with the fall.
Crinkled edges began to sing,
"Knock knock! Who's there?"—just a tree wing.

Wrapped in sunlight, it twirled and spun,
Lounging with shadows, oh, what fun!
"Hey, leaf, don't forget your shade!"
"We strive to be fierce, we too have made!"

Seasons wove on, each a quick glance,
As puddles giggled, "Join us in dance!"
Life's a parade, short and sweet,
Even roots can tap to the beat!

At last, it fell, with a cheeky grin,
"Thank you, dear tree, for all that's been!"
And though it's scattered, don't shed a tear,
For laughter's the fabric that brings us near.

Stories of Starlight

Beneath an oak, a leaf would sway,
With stories to tell of the sun's play.
"I flew with the birds, oh what a flight!
We raced through sunsets, oh, what a sight!"

Then in the dark, it giggled low,
"Fireflies wink, put on a show!"
"I've got tales of the moonlit night,
And a soft breeze that felt just right!"

But time marched on with heedless feet,
"Hey leaf, hold tight, don't face defeat!"
Yet each fall cracked a laugh so loud,
Nature's confetti, all so proud!

So when it landed on soil anew,
It whispered secrets to the dew.
For every twist, every giggle gained,
Leaves of the past are still unchained!

The Leaf's Leavetaking

Once bright and green, now turning brown,
It's hard to face the wind, don't frown.
A gust comes by, I'm feeling spry,
Flipping like a pancake, oh my!

I danced on branches, a playful twirl,
Now I'm on the ground, let fate unfurl.
A kid runs by, I hear a squeal,
Catching me, oh what a deal!

With every stomp, I feel the fun,
Crushed and crinkled, but I won't run.
Laughter echoes as I take a dive,
In this funny chaos, I'm alive!

So here's my farewell, as I drift away,
Rolling on the pavement, it's a leaf's play.
A leaf's last dance, a comical spree,
Nature's way of laughing with glee!

Invisible Webs of Life

Oh look at me, I'm stuck on a thread,
A spider's web? I'm shaking my head!
Swinging like a swing, caught in the glee,
Not quite the freedom I thought I'd see!

Moths flutter by in the moonlit night,
I wave hello, they give me a fright.
Who knew I'd end up a webbed fool?
Dinner plans, I'm not looking so cool!

I tell my pals, 'We'll float like a breeze,'
But here I am, as snack for the bees.
Life has its traps, oh what a twist,
Invisible webs, here's my funny list!

So while I dangle in this quirky state,
Spinning my story, I'll just wait.
With a chuckle, I embrace the plight,
In the dance of life, I'll shine so bright!

Glints of Golden Sunlight

Basked in warmth, a bright delight,
I soak up rays, what a sunny sight!
Chasing shadows, we play peek-a-boo,
I'm a golden star, all fresh and new!

The morning dew, my sparkling dress,
Wobbling softly, I must confess.
A butterfly flutters, puts on a show,
We giggle and sway, 'Come dance with us, yo!'

But watch out for clouds that look so gray,
They sneak up on us, ruin our play.
I'll have a meltdown, it's just so cruel,
Nature's drama—it's nobody's fool!

So here's to the laughs in the golden light,
Chasing rainbows, taking flight.
Each glint a giggle, each ray a cheer,
Living this life, with no hint of fear!

Cherished Moments in Green

In the grand old tree, we sway and sing,
Oh, what joy the seasons bring!
Swinging with friends in the gentle breeze,
Life's little moments, a joyful tease!

We tell tall tales of storms and rain,
When squirrels play tag and never complain.
They scurry and dart, we cheer from above,
Nature's characters, it's all turtle love!

Under the sun, we throw shade and grin,
Every rustle's a giggle, where do I begin?
A sudden gust makes us shimmy and shake,
Oh what a life, cuts through the ache!

With whispers of laughter, we dance in line,
In this green paradise, everything's fine.
Those cherished moments we love to glean,
Oh, the hilarity in all that's green!

Biography of a Breath of Air

Once a sprightly puff of fun,
Dancing through the rays of sun.
Tickled by the laughter of trees,
Whispering secrets in the breeze.

With a hop and a skip I fly,
Over rooftops, low and high.
Sometimes I swirl, sometimes I dive,
Trying to make the world come alive.

I tickle noses, ruffle hair,
No one seems to mind or care.
But watch me sneak into a sneeze,
A little chaos, if you please!

In this great air dance I reside,
Full of giggles and playful pride.
I trace the paths of every glee,
Life's hilarious dance, oh so free!

Palette of Nature's Canvas

There's a painter up in the sky,
Swirling shades as time goes by.
With splashes of yellow, red, and green,
Creating scenes like you've never seen.

Leaves join in, a comical crowd,
Waving and flapping, feeling proud.
They shimmy on branches, do a jig,
Trying to fit in, but oh so big!

With a gust comes a splendid show,
Colors twirl and spin below.
Nature chuckles, what a sight,
Painting the world from morning to night!

And when it rains, they laugh even more,
Splashing about on the forest floor.
Artistry lives in every breeze,
Where nature laughs and never flees!

Surrendering to the Chill

When frosty whispers take their hold,
I giggle and shiver, feeling bold.
Twirling down from branches bare,
Trying to dance without a care.

Winter's breath, oh what a tease,
I flutter down with utmost ease.
Plopping on the ground in glee,
Becoming part of the cold marquee!

Wearing blankets of glimmering white,
I tell the world, 'What a delight!'
Frosty spectacles twinkle and play,
While I lounge around, happy to stay.

Cozying up, I share some grins,
As the snowman spins with goofy spins.
In this chilly realm I cheerfully rest,
For laughter and fun are truly the best!

Mosaics of a Shifting Sky

Up above, what a sight to see,
Clouds dance like they're on a spree.
Shapes of bunnies and fluffs of cream,
All the while, they giggle and beam.

As they shift and change in the day,
I try to guess what they will play.
Perhaps a dragon, or a silly hat,
Nature's art, can you believe that?

The sun sneaks in with a cheeky grin,
Lighting the sky where the fun begins.
Stars come out just to twinkle and tease,
To play hide and seek amongst the trees.

Through storms they rumble, laugh and shout,
Never afraid to twist and twout.
In this gallery of skies so bright,
Life's funny quirks bring pure delight!

The Quiet Farewell of Green

In the breeze, I wave goodbye,
Hiding laughter, not a sigh.
It's my time to turn on red,
As the autumn paints my bed.

Squirrels scamper, gather fast,
Thinking I won't be their last.
But I chuckle, drifting down,
A leafy jester, wearing brown.

Floating down with twirls and spins,
In this game, no one wins.
But the ground awaits my grace,
Join the pile, it's a warm embrace.

Oh, the stories we will share,
With the wind tousling my hair.
From my perch, I bid adieu,
Smirking at the skies so blue.

Transitions of Time: A Leaf's Perspective

Born in spring, I danced with glee,
Soaking up the sun, carefree.
But oh the days start racing past,
Waving goodbye, I've had a blast.

Summer's heat, I bake and fry,
Complaining softly, "Oh my, why?"
Then comes fall, my color show,
Reds and yellows, off I go!

"Winter's coming!" chirp the birds,
My fate's sealed, without any words.
I'll spin and twist on chilly nights,
Like a dancer, reaching heights!

A final flip onto the ground,
My laughter echoes all around.
Time's a riot, full of pranks,
In the end, we'll share our thanks!

The Stories Held in Veins

My veins run tales of sun and shade,
Of breezy nights when I delayed.
A heart so thin, yet full of cheer,
I hold the whispers of the year.

Once a tiny bud, I took the leap,
In the sun's light, I'd take a peep.
Through funny storms and playful gales,
I ride the winds, I tell the tales.

Colors change, a wacky game,
Mimicking the clouds, never the same.
I weave through seasons, I sway and glide,
A comedic journey that I ride.

With a laugh, I start to fall,
Joining others in a grassy hall.
Stories continue without a trace,
For every leaf finds its own space.

Beneath the Canopy: A Leaf's Journey

Beneath this vast green canopy,
I have my dreams, oh can it be?
With every flicker, I wave hello,
To the critters down below.

I heard a rumor, a funny jest,
That branches grow, but leaves do best!
Hiding among the joyful throngs,
I sway to nature's silly songs.

I dodge the raindrops, do a twist,
Evade the storms, I can't resist!
Each day a giggle, a leap of faith,
In this leafy world, I'm never wraith.

But soon the skies will signal change,
To pack my bags, no time to arrange!
I'll tumble down, with a wink and spin,
A playful exit, let the fun begin!

The Colorful Chronicles

In spring I'm bright, a joyous green,
I dance with flowers, a leafy queen.
But then I see a squirrel so spry,
He leaps and nearly makes me cry!

Come summer's heat, I turn to gold,
My stories of sunbeams are proudly told.
Yet a raindrop splashes with a funny splat,
I giggle at nature, how silly is that!

As autumn calls, I twist and swirl,
In a whimsical dance, oh what a whirl!
But I get stuck in a grumpy old boot,
And laugh as I wiggle, oh how cute!

When winter's chill wraps me tight,
I think of summers, oh what a sight!
With frost I'm frosty, but I don't mind,
I'm the quirkiest leaf, one of a kind!

Symphony of Sunlight

The sun shines bright, I catch its rays,
I flip and flop in a leafy ballet.
Birds chirp tunes while I sway with glee,
This giggly show is quite a sight to see!

In the breeze I flutter, a carefree waltz,
But I trip on a twig and it really halts.
I tumble down, with a hilarious flail,
Landing on a snail who tells a tall tale!

As shadows fall, I join a parade,
With ants and bugs, it's a grand charade.
We gather 'round to play leaf tag,
My friends all laugh, while I just sag!

Though seasons change and colors fade,
I treasure the laughs, the joy we made.
With each funny fling, I feel so alive,
A quirky old leaf, just happy to thrive!

Conversations with the Breeze

Oh breezy friend, come talk with me,
We giggle about clouds and the sun's decree.
You tease my edges with a playful spin,
I wobble and wobble, where to begin?

We talk of sunshine, of stormy fright,
You say I'm your favorite, what a delight!
But when the rain comes, it gets so slick,
I slip and slide, oh what a trick!

As winds grow wild, I take to the air,
Twisting and turning without a care.
Until I land in a puddle quite deep,
I chuckle at splashes—oh, what a leap!

Together we dance in the balmy dusk,
You share all your secrets, I unlock the rust.
Through life's funny moments, a blend of ease,
Forever we'll chatter, just you and the trees!

The Unraveling Edges

I'm crinkled and curled at the tips, you see,
Life's little frays, oh woe is me!
But then here comes a caterpillar so plump,
He munches my edges with a little thump!

In spring I was perfect, a proud, sharp cut,
Now I'm a buffoon with edges that rut.
A gust sends me tumbling, I shout 'Hey there!'
I'm more interesting now—I've got flair!

As seasons keep changing, I'll shed my disguise,
Chasing the wind, I'll reach for the skies.
With every mishap, a laugh I will share,
For life's funny moments are the light in the air!

So here's to the fraying, the funny and bold,
Each twist and turn, a story retold.
With every adventure, my spirit won't tire,
I'm the jester of nature, my edges on fire!

Golden Tales Under the Canopy

In the shade where stories grow,
Frogs in tuxedos put on a show.
Squirrels gossip about acorn wealth,
While dandelions flaunt their stealth.

Dancing shadows, they twist and twirl,
A ladybug spins in a dizzy whirl.
Ticklish breezes tickle the trees,
As the sun sneezes, "Ah-choo!" with ease.

Jumpy rabbits play tag with the breeze,
While grasshoppers knock knees for a tease.
A caterpillar dreams of flights so grand,
But first, he must keep his band!

Laughter echoes through branches high,
As clouds drift by in a silly sky.
Golden tales under the canopy,
Where giggles reign with pure glee!

Grasping the Wind's Embrace

I hang from a branch, swaying in delight,
Chasing the breeze with all of my might.
A gust blows strong; oh, what fun it seems,
I twirl around, dancing in dreams.

With every gust, I pull a funny face,
Pretending to race in this wild place.
The wind whispers secrets in my ear,
While I giggle, 'Hey, did you hear?'

Birds look on with bewildered beaks,
Wondering what this leaf speaks.
But I'm just here to spin and prance,
Grasping the wind's silly dance.

As autumn arrives with a raucous cheer,
I'll float down softly, without any fear.
In the laughter of nature, I'll find my space,
With friends made of soil, I'll embrace!

The Elegy of Shimmering Color

Once I was green, full of sass,
Now I'm a hue, bold but alas!
I crack jokes with sunbeams above,
As I twirl in a whirlwind of love.

Orange snaps and red pops like a joke,
Each hue a meme as the fall winds stoke.
I hear chuckles from branches so wide,
Even the clouds can't keep their pride.

"Look at me!" I croak as I shed,
While butterflies dance in filament threads.
Unlike my pals, I'm destined to roam,
As drifting laughter leads me home.

So here's to the colors that come and sway,
With a wink and a nod, I'll find my way.
An elegy sung, not for sorrow's grace,
But a ripple of joy in this vibrant space!

Rustling Secrets of the Woodlands

In a world where whispers softly scheme,
The wind and I plot our grandest dream.
I rustle up tales that tickle the pine,
While chattering chipmunks sip on brine.

Owls hoot giggles from high above,
As sticks complain, half in love.
Wildflowers dress with a playful swoosh,
While ants form a line with a silly whoosh.

"I'm just a leaf!" I cry with glee,
"But in this world, I feel so free!"
Secrets rustle secrets, so dapper and neat,
Under the canopy, life's a grand treat.

So let's tumble together till dusk settles low,
For the woodlands hold stories that endlessly flow.
In every rustle, listen close and see,
That laughter is hidden in each leafy spree!

Interlude of Ephemeral Beauty

In the breeze, I do a dance,
Flipping, flopping, no second chance.
One moment grand, the next I'm down,
A twirling, whirling leaf-shaped clown.

Colors flash, I'm quite the sight,
Orange, yellow, all bold and bright.
But down I go, a bit of a flop,
And hope a squirrel doesn't want to stop.

Caught in a gust, I fly with glee,
Waving to birds, they laugh at me.
I nearly land on a sleeping dog,
He snorts and rolls, what a funny fog!

But as I drift, I'm not worried,
Confetti of trees, a party I'm hurried.
For every fall, a tale to tell,
In my short life, I dance quite well!

Touching the Ground

I tumbled down from my lofty throne,
A leaf's journey, forever prone.
With a little spin and a flippity flap,
I end up crumpled, what a mishap!

Upon the ground, I see the ants,
Marching along in ridiculous pants.
They look up at me, so full of cheer,
But I just think, 'What brought me here?'

Oh, the fun of resting in dirt,
A cozy bed, but oh, the hurt!
I once was high, now I'm part of the floor,
With a ladybug nodding, 'You were a bore!'

Yet laughter echoes, as I embrace this fate,
Gazing at clouds, growing quite late.
From lofty heights to this earthy spread,
I'm just a funny fellow; I'm not yet dead!

Melodies from the Canopy

Up in the trees, I sway to the song,
Birds are my buddies, we're all getting along.
With a flap and a chirp, we're quite the band,
Life is a concert, and I'm in demand!

Rustling rhythms in the balmy air,
My neighbors, the branches, swing without care.
Have you tried to shimmy in a breeze?
T'was a leaf's party, come join if you please!

But as I groove, I feel a slight rip,
The wind gives a pull, and I start to dip.
"Hold on tight!" I yell to my friends,
Until gravity says, "This fun simply ends!"

As I swirl down, I laugh out loud,
Landed on grass, amidst a crowd.
Though the music fades in this leafy retreat,
The memories dance—oh, life is sweet!

Organic Orations

Gather 'round, I have tales galore,
Of sun-kissed days and winds that roar.
I might be green, but I'm wise, it's true,
A leaf philosopher, who knew?

"Listen close," I start with flair,
"Life's funny games, an elaborate dare.
One moment you're swaying, the next you're toast,
Oh, how we giggle, I shall boast!"

Sharing wisdom with the vines at my side,
Riddles of nature, a comical ride.
"Why did the twig refuse to dance?
Because it couldn't take a chance!"

Laughter rings out throughout the trees,
While critters join in, they're aiming to please.
So come, take a seat on this leafy throne,
For stories and giggles are never alone!

Cradled in Nature's Arms

In the cradle of trees, I sway with glee,
A dance on the breeze, just you and me.
I tickle the squirrel, I tease the dear,
With whispers of rustles, I sing in cheer.

I've dodged raindrops, they wanted to cling,
Made friends with a snail, he thinks I'm a king.
I play hide and seek with the sun's warm glow,
Waving at clouds as they put on a show.

My bright green jacket's the talk of the park,
I'm the life of the party, a leaf with a spark.
But now I'm all wrinkled, what can I say?
Life's funny that way, just a leaf gone astray.

As seasons turn round, I splatter and spin,
In a whirl of confetti, my journey begins.
But I won't be a bother, I won't make a fuss,
Just landing on shoulders, I'm famous, you trust!

The Fall's Gentle Farewell

When autumn arrives, I turn shades of gold,
A dazzling display, if I may be so bold.
I wave goodbye to branches, my friends up high,
With a flip and a twirl, off I tiptoe and fly.

I land on a puddle, make ripples with style,
A splash of laughter that stretches a mile.
The kids all come running, they want a leaf race,
I'm the star of the show, can't keep up with my pace!

I settle on shoulders of munchkins below,
As they stomp through the grasses, so lively, you know.
I giggle in breezes, a jolly delight,
A merry old wanderer, I dance through the night.

With friends all around me, it's a whimsical blast,
Swirling and twirling, we're having a blast.
Though winter is coming, I'll never be sad,
For memories are treasures, as funny as glad!

Verdant Chronicles in the Sun

In the sun's warm embrace, I write my tale,
Adventures of bouncing in the warm summer gale.
From morning's first light till the dusk's final buzz,
I'm the lively companion of all that is fuzz.

I met a fast bug who thought he could race,
But I'm catching the breeze, so he's lost in space.
With ants on parade, we formed quite the crew,
The mischief we stirred, oh, if only you knew!

A twist and a twirl, my life's quite absurd,
I often play tag with the shy little bird.
I'm the leaf they call crazy, with quips that entice,
On the branches above, we roll the dice.

But as sunshine fades, and shadows creep near,
I'll poke fun at the stars in the sky up here.
Embracing the night, I shout out my cheer,
Just a leaf full of joy, it's great to be here!

Petals and Shadows Intertwined

In a garden of giggles, I swish and I sway,
With petals around me, we laugh and play.
The flowers all tease as I flutter and flap,
"You're the light-footed jester, you fell from my lap!"

Shadows stretch long with a wink from the moon,
While crickets provide a night-time cartoon.
I'm the lovable prankster, just perched on a stem,
Every breeze brings laughter, I'm laughing with them.

With whispers of pollen, we dance in the air,
Mixing up chuckles, we start the affair.
A dance with the shadows, a tryst on the lawn,
A party of petals from dusk until dawn.

When morning arrives, we'll shake off the zany,
Embracing the sunlight, we'll renew the crazy.
For once there was twirling, now there's boisterous glee,
A leaf in a garden — it's fun being me!

Sunlit Dreams in the Breeze

Dancing high in the cheerful sky,
I wave to the ants hustling by.
Swirling with giggles, a wild little twirl,
A sunbeam's tickle makes me whirl!

Caught on a nose of a passing pup,
Spun through the air—oh, what a jump!
Daring to ride a curious breeze,
I'm off to chase clouds, if you please!

With whispers of joy that only I hear,
The laughter of sunlight brings me cheer.
I twinkle down to a puddle below,
And leap in the water—oh, what a show!

Soon I shall revel in hues of the fall,
While causing a ruckus, I'll try not to stall.
As the seasons twist in a comical way,
I'll bid the world farewell—here I sway!

From Buds to Crumbles

I sprouted so proudly, a glorious green,
In parks where I danced, a sight seldom seen.
With a crown of bright dew, I took my stand,
But soon came the munchies—oh, wasn't it grand!

From yummy young buds to zesty old fate,
I chuckled, "Oh dear, I'm just the right plate!"
The caterpillars tickled; I giggled with glee,
Not for a moment, was I worried, you see!

With every crisp crunch, I played my part well,
Fulfilling their cravings, oh who could rebel?
Yet here comes the breeze, taking me near,
As I tumble and twist with nary a fear!

From being a treat to a crumbling joke,
The wind parts my friends, with a gentle poke.
Laughter erupts as I float to the ground,
A comical dance with no care all around!

Echoes of a Season's Change

In spring I wore green, a vibrant delight,
With dew drop diamonds that shone very bright.
I twirled on the branches, carefree and bold,
But waited for more—life's stories unfold!

Then summer arrived, and what did I seek?
A sunbath of joy on my skin was unique.
I laughed as I fluttered, with friends all around,
While the bees shared their stories, the sweetest sound.

But autumn laughed loud, with colors so grand,
I dressed in the reds that life had planned.
The wind called my name, and I spun with delight,
Adventuring bravely into the night!

As winter approached, I rustled with cheer,
Pondering how cute I'd look, have no fear.
Though I might get crunchy, and crumble with ease,
Life's merely a giggle in the cozy of freeze!

A Leaf's Silent Soliloquy

Oh, what a sight as I sway on my twig,
A silent observer, all jolly and big.
With whispers of winds that tickle my base,
I giggle to see nature's funny face!

I watch as the squirrels bound out of sight,
With nuts in their cheeks, what a comical sight!
Their acorn chases, a comedic dance,
While I chuckle from up high, in my leafy romance.

The seasons all change, I feel myself fade,
From vibrant to crispy, oh, what a trade!
But laughter endures in this comely fall,
As I glide gently down, I'll answer the call.

For each little crunch and the crinkle they make,
Brings joy to the children, a giggly mistake.
Though my time here is brief, in the sun's merry glow,
I bloom one last chuckle—so down I will go!

From Green to Golden

Once a sprout, bright and gay,
Dancing in the sun's warm ray.
Now I've turned from green to gold,
Playing peek-a-boo, so bold.

Wind whispers jokes on high,
Telling tales as I wave goodbye.
I'll twirl down to the ground, you see,
To make a pile for kids with glee.

Squirrels laugh as they dive and dive,
Into my pile where they arrive.
Leaves like me, a comical crew,
Who knew falling could be so true?

I might just grace a pumpkin's hat,
Or flutter like a scrappy mat.
From tree to earth, it's quite a spree,
Living life so joyfully!

A Sentence Written in Chlorophyll

In a book of sunlit dreams,
I pen my thoughts in leafy beams.
Every whisper is a rhyme,
Crafted slowly, taking time.

Oh, to bask in summer's light,
Ink of green, it feels just right.
Every drop of morning dew,
Jots my tales, so fresh, so new.

Then comes autumn, a plot twist fair,
Suddenly, my words lay bare.
No more sentences so bright,
Just a script of brownish fright.

Yet laughter echoes in the breeze,
As I play with gusts with ease.
A sentence written without care,
Leaves my thoughts dancing in the air!

The Poetry of Decay

Once so lush, now a crunchy mess,
Time to revel in my distress.
A poet at my end of days,
I sing of slipping in funny ways.

Cracking jokes on a chilly night,
Termites cackle, oh what a sight!
Each crumbly line a laugh, a cheer,
The punchline's sharp, it draws you near.

As I tumble, oh what a ride,
Worms find solace, I'm their pride.
In my fragments, they take a bite,
Dining on my fading light.

Yet through decay, I'll find a muse,
In every shard, a laugh I'll choose.
Life's a jest, both bright and bleak,
In my downfall, comedy we seek!

Celestial Calligraphy

Dancing stars in the autumn sky,
I'm a script of nature flying high.
Each twirl a line, each spin a dot,
Writing patterns in the parking lot.

A comet zips, I take my cue,
Scrawling trails, oh look at me too!
With every gust I draft a new verse,
Nature's penmanship, quite diverse.

Fellows giggle at my descent,
Creating art with every event.
With the breeze, my words take flight,
In swirling chaos, oh so bright.

So here I float, a playful draft,
A cosmic joke, a greenish craft.
In the air, I softly scrawl,
A masterpiece for one and all!

www.ingramcontent.com/pod-product-compliance
Lightning Source LLC
Chambersburg PA
CBHW050317100526
44585CB00016BA/1565